The Batsford Book of
Britain in colour

The Batsford Book of Britain in colour

Introduction by WALTER ALLEN

with notes on the plates by

FRANCIS MAXWELL

B. T. BATSFORD LTD LONDON

First published 1965
Fourth Impression 1976
New Edition 1981

© B. T. Batsford Ltd 1981

Printed in Hong Kong
for The Publishers
B. T. BATSFORD LTD
4 Fitzhardinge Street, London W1H 0AH

ISBN 0 7134 3504 6

The Plates

THE PLATES

THE PLATES

Introduction

GEORGE BORROW, a great traveller if ever there was one, said: 'There are no countries less known by the British than those self-same British Islands.' But that was rather more than a hundred years ago, and things are different now. Within a generation of Borrow's writing, the railway train had made us all trippers, and now, what with cars and planes, universal education and holidays with pay, we are all tourists, whether at home or abroad. All the same, when I look at the photographs in this book, which could be multiplied a hundred times without losing their representative quality, I feel some dismay and even shame as I realise how much of the British Isles I have not yet seen. The shame is irrational. It is impossible to go everywhere, see everything, and one wants and needs to see other countries as well as one's own. But beyond that is the simple fact that it would be impossible in a single life-time for anyone except a professional traveller, a Borrow perhaps, to see everything Britain has to offer.

On the face of it, it may seem strange that this should be so. Britain is not a large country. But it is an extremely diversified one, in scenery, landscape, styles of architecture. It is this that always hits me, for it always comes again as a surprise, whenever I return from abroad, the sense of how quickly everything changes as one travels a relatively few miles, the sense of how much variety is packed into so small a space. I have lived for some months more or less on the banks of the Hudson River in New York State and travelled often on the roads and railways that parallel its course. The Hudson and the valley through which it flows are astonishingly beautiful; they exist on the grand romantic

9

INTRODUCTION

scale as nothing in Britain south of the Scottish Highlands can be
said to do; and one has only to lift one's eyes from the four-lane
highway that flanks the river to think one is still in Fenimore
Cooper's country, in the land of the last of the Mohicans. But—
and this is my present point—the nature of the landscape scarcely
changes throughout the hundred-and-fifty miles from New York
to Albany. One remains as it were in the same unit of landscape,
and it is a continental unit. I have never travelled those miles
without thinking how in Britain, traversing a similar distance, I
would have passed through a dozen different landscapes, one
might say almost a dozen different histories.

Yet it may still seem strange that so much remains that is not-
able in Britain, so much worth travelling thousands of miles to
see, for Britain is not only a small country, it is also a very highly
industrialised one. You will not find evidence of it in this book;
for a good reason. If you spend your working life in Birmingham,
England, or Birmingham, Alabama, in St Helen's, Lancashire or
Newark, New Jersey, in Lille, France, or Krefeld, Germany, it is
unlikely that you will wish to take your holidays in Sheffield or
Liverpool or Newcastle-upon-Tyne, though all three cities have
fine things to see in them. The truth is, the industrial landscape
has become the one international landscape, as predictable from
country to country, as alike, as airports are. You don't need to
come to Britain to see it, though once you did, for it was in
Britain two centuries ago, in Glasgow, in Birmingham and the
nearby 'Black Country', and in the Potteries thirty miles to the
north, that the industrial revolution began. Once it was new and,

10

to the outsider, whether a Londoner like Charles Dickens or a foreigner, it was horrifying. In 1861, the American historian Henry Adams, then a young man just out of Harvard, came to England to join his father, the American Minister at the Court of St James. Years later, in his classic autobiography, *The Education of Henry Adams*, he remembered his journey by train south from Liverpool:

> Then came the journey up to London through Birmingham and the Black District, another lesson, which needed much more to be rightly felt. This plunge into darkness lurid with flames; the sense of unknown horror in the weird gloom which then existed nowhere else, and never existed before, except in volcanic craters; the violent contrast between the dense, smoky, impenetrable darkness, and the soft green that one glided into —the revelation of the unknown society of the pit—made a boy uncomfortable, though he had no idea that Karl Marx was standing by waiting for him, and that sooner or later the process of education would have to deal with Karl Marx much more than with Professor Bowen of Harvard College or his Satanic free-trade majesty John Stuart Mill. The Black District was a practical education, but it was infinitely far in the future. The boy ran away from it, as he ran away from everything he disliked.

'Gloom which then existed nowhere else, and never had existed before.' Well, the industrial landscape that so repelled the young

INTRODUCTION

Adams as he travelled the thirteen miles from Wolverhampton to Birmingham is now reproduced and intensified and multiplied in the view from the train as you travel the ten-times-greater distance from New York through New Jersey to Philadelphia; and I have stood in the centre of the town of Moravska-Ostrova in Czechoslovakia and could almost have sworn I was in Smethwick, Staffordshire, three miles from where I was born.

So, in a book of this kind, pictures of industrial Britain are unnecessary and uncalled for; to include them would be merely to carry coals to the majority of readers' private and local Newcastles. Yet for me it is impossible to look at these pictures or to see what they represent in actuality without making the silent reference back to the British industrial scene. For two reasons. It is the technological revolution, of which industrialism is one aspect, that has made it possible for the enormous majority of us, the mass of citizens of the western world, to be tourists at all. If the inhabitants of Borrow's British Islands did not know those selfsame British Islands it was because it was not in their power to do so. They had, most of them, neither the money nor the means of transport: when your only method of locomotion is your own two legs you stay where you are. We are all dependent for the means of travel that we now take for granted upon the industrialism in which most of us live and from which, reasonably, we aim to get away when on holiday. But it is also the very fact that we live in overwhelmingly industrial environments that draws us to their opposite, to scenes and places far removed in time, mood and pace of living. We are all romantics nowadays, and it is industrialism that has largely made us so.

As must be apparent, I am a townee, the offspring of three generations of townees. I do not regret that I was born and spent the formative years of my life in Birmingham, a city that is almost entirely a nineteenth-century creation and the centre of an industrial conurbation of five million people, a wen considerably greater than London was when Cobbett first applied the word to it. The experience of growing up in a densely populated industrial area has shaped me. Inevitably, it predisposed me to see the industrial scene as the natural habitat of man. For me as a child the country was so different from, other than, the city as to exist almost in opposition to it; the country was automatically foreign country. And yet—it is plain now, looking back—the mind demanded more. I remember as a boy wandering through the region of the north-west of Birmingham, in the no-man's-land between Birmingham and the Black Country, looking Saturday night after Saturday night for something I could identify as beautiful, the beautiful, you understand, in industrial terms. Saturday night after Saturday night I found it. But what seems to me significant now is that it was at night I found it. What I was really doing was interpreting the industrial landscape through the French Impressionist painters I had recently discovered. It was the French Impressionists and their literary kinsmen the Naturalists who first sought and found beauty in the industrial landscape, by emphasising the play of light on the urban scene. My mentors, besides the painters, were novelists like Arnold Bennett, who had similarly been brought up in an industrial region, and one not far away from mine, and for whom it was urgently necessary to find in his industrial region something recognisable as beauty; for the mind demands beauty, and beauty near at hand.

We all start from our first environment, the place where we were born, and I was bringing what I now see as a naturally romantic imagination to my initial surroundings. They had, somehow, to be made imaginatively acceptable. I was, too, obsessed by the division and the contrast, the division and the contrast between the industrial landscape that was home and what lay magically outside it, the country, the other, which I suppose was a symbol of innocence, almost of the world before the Fall. There were glimpses of this even within the confines of the city itself, for, less than two miles from its centre, bang up against Aston Villa Football Club, Birmingham has one of the finest Elizabethan manor houses, Aston Hall. I admire it more now than I did as a child, when it had the quality of a familiar freak. There was, I seem to remember, the back-bone of a whale in the entrance hall: it was, in fact, the overflow from the city museum; and I looked elsewhere.

I looked—and if you live in Birmingham you can hardly help looking towards them—to Warwick and Stratford-upon-Avon, neither much more than twenty miles away. Their very closeness to Birmingham was part of their fascination, which was that of the ultimate contrast with my Victorian environment. Warwick, with its historic castle and the ruins of another, Kenilworth, not far away, is one of the finest medieval towns in Britain; and as for Stratford, hadn't Shakespeare been born and lived there? When

Shakespeare was a boy Birmingham was an unimportant market-town: I used to wonder whether the boy Shakespeare had ever visited it, as two centuries after him Dr Johnson as a boy had walked thither from Lichfield. The very notion that he might have done gave my native city some kind of cachet. Warwick and Stratford today, in terms of real estate, are commuters' suburbs of Birmingham; yet they body forth, however more grandly, what Birmingham itself once was, and for me as a boy they represented a Warwickshire past to which I, because I was born in Warwickshire, belonged. By visiting them, by identifying myself with them, I came into part of my rightful heritage.

And perhaps this throws light on industrial Britain and the other older, apparently very different Britain in which it exists. They do not, after all, exist in such stark opposition as I believed once upon a time. The new—or the comparatively new—does not necessarily destroy the old—or the comparatively old. If the industrial areas appear as so many blots on the face of Britain then they do so as blots on a much-scored palimpsest: they hide but do not obliterate what lies beneath them. And—to keep to the image —they are not of uniform thickness or blackness. At times they thin out to little more than a slight smear. Often, indeed, they look much worse than they actually are: one mustn't be deceived by the industrial smoke that covers them; it is often nothing more than protective coloration. The greatest centre of industry in the west country, Bristol, for all its acres on acres of aeroplane factories and Victorian terrace-houses, its appallingly undistinguished centre, is still one of the richest and most rewarding of British cities, with the Regency squares and crescents of Clifton, its downs and the superb gorge of the Avon spanned by Brunel's bridge.

Even where industry is at its most concentrated it is still rare for those who live among it to be more than a few miles from the countryside. Often it is there almost at the back door. One thinks of Sheffield, set in its wild moors and with the mountainous Peak district of Derbyshire at hand, or of Bradford, with Haworth and the bleak high country of Emily Brontë's *Wuthering Heights* not far away, or of Glasgow, with the glory of the Trossachs at hand and the legend-steeped Highlands and the Western Isles in reach.

I have said that we are all tourists nowadays, and I notice that, to illustrate the usage of the word, *The Concise Oxford Dictionary* had the following: 'The place is overrun with tourists.' Tourists, one might say, are people from the outside world who come to look but rarely stay to linger, for they are prisoners of the means of transport which has brought tourism into being. Now the Briton on holiday in Britain is as much a tourist as any visiting foreigner, as much the sight-seer, as a general rule, from a world outside. The only thing that prevents us from realising this is the word Britain itself, which is not so much a country as a geographical expression, or, if it is a country, is still an artificial entity made up of countries that differ radically from one another in history, traditions, habits of speech, and sometimes even language itself. These countries, moreover, are themselves made up of sharply differing regions in which the Englishman —Scotsman—Welshman—Irishman—from one among them may easily feel himself a foreigner in the others.

16

INTRODUCTION

I am the more acutely conscious of this because I, an Englishman, am writing these words in the city of Edinburgh. It is one of the most beautiful and most fantastic cities in the world, and I can never visit it without being struck again by its foreignness, by which I mean its utter unlikeness to any English city I know. Even those features of it which stem from English influences have been transmuted into something quite different. The New Town, for example. The source of its inspiration is obvious—the Georgian city of Bath; but, built in granite, the Georgian houses, squares and crescents of the New Town have a dourness, an uncompromising hardness, that give them a dignity and austerity, an almost Roman austerity, beyond anything that Bath, set in the lush green hills of Avon, possesses. What one thinks of as a characteristically English style of domestic architecture has been translated perfectly into a medium one feels to be native, as perfectly, though how differently, as Georgian was translated into Colonial in the thirteen colonies that became the United States.

And the New Town derives from England! Nothing else in Edinburgh does. Its geography, the hills around it, the buildings on the hills and the cleft between the New Town and the Old, in which there was once a lake and through which the railway now runs, all conspire to suggest both Prague and a blackened, altogether grimmer Athens. These are, perhaps, chance resemblances, but the foreignness of Edinburgh to my English eyes is not due to them. Take the castle that dominates the city. It stands above the Mound as a symbol of strength, of domination: who holds the Castle holds Edinburgh. But the first thing that impresses me about it is that it is not an English castle; at any rate, I know of no castle in England like it. But I have seen similar castles rising out of the plain of Hungary.

Nor is this all. Place names, street names, the speech of the people, these too help to make me feel a foreigner, i.e., excluded from a shared way of life, when I am in Edinburgh. It is not important that the shop assistants and bus conductors do not easily understand my accent, or I theirs; this might be the case in Devon or Dorset. Much more important is that educated Scots, who do understand me, speak an English that is not mine and is in many respects more different from the English of England than is that of the United States. There are Scots by the thousand in England —what did Dr Johnson say about the Scotsman's noblest prospect?—but at home the Scottishness of my Scots friends is something I am hardly more aware of than the Yorkshireness of my friends from Yorkshire. Scots in England merge into the local scene. Perhaps an essence becomes diluted. But go to Edinburgh, and all is different. One is conscious all about one of national types, set apart from the English by subtle though quite clear differences of physique, facial contours, colour of hair and complexion. One is, quite simply, in Scotland, not in a deviation from an English norm but in another norm, one existing in its own right without reference to England, except as to the hereditary enemy and still, perhaps, as the absent-minded oppressor.

Above all, what impresses me when I am in Edinburgh, or anywhere else in Scotland that I know, is the feeling that I am in the presence of a wholly distinct past, a different history, one, moreover, that is often scarcely distinguishable from legend; a history characterised by violence of a scale and of an intensity unknown in England for more than three centuries and much nearer the surface, much nearer the present, than anything one experiences south of the border.

This is, admittedly, an Englishman's romantic view of Scotland, but I do not apologise for it, since what is it except romanticism, the appeal of the strange, the novel, the exotic, of all the qualities that are different from those that make up our day-to-day environments, that sends us pouring out of our home-towns by the million year after year like lemmings? And if, for the Englishman touring the British Isles, Scotland is an extreme case, it is not the only one. Certainly no more extreme than that of Ireland, where a violent history presses even more insistently into the near-present; and hardly more foreign than parts of Wales, where, as an undergraduate, I used to walk because it was the nearest country where a foreign language was spoken.

'What ought we to see when we come to Britain?' Nothing brings one up more abruptly against one's ignorance of one's own country than this question put to one so often by some many friends abroad. More than half of my life has been based on London—and I have never penetrated the Tower, climbed the Monument, watched the Changing of the Guard or seen the Lord Mayor's Show. And indeed, except in the most general terms, the question is unanswerable. Of a dozen cathedrals, how choose one in preference to another? Why do I always wistfully hope that my friends will go to see Lichfield Cathedral? The reason is subjective,

INTRODUCTION

and again it goes back to my boyhood in Birmingham. Lichfield was my first introduction to history in the sense of continuity made visible in a specific building. Again, I discovered there the past that had been all but blotted out in my surroundings; all but —for the past remained in place-names. The names of such Black Country towns as Wolverhampton, Kingswinford and Wednesbury take one straight back to Anglo-Saxon England, indeed to pre-Christian England, to the ancient kingdom of Mercia. But only the names; whereas in Lichfield, a dozen or so miles away but outside the blackness, it wasn't difficult to feel oneself back in a remote past. The cathedral dates from the fourteenth century, but the city has been the seat of a bishopric since the seventh, the first bishop being the Anglo-Saxon St Chad, to whom the cathedral is dedicated.

Whether these private associations of mine with Lichfield justify my sending foreign friends to visit the ancient city I don't know. If they go, they won't be wasting their time: Lichfield is one of the most beautiful of the smaller English cathedrals, and then there is the city's most famous son, Dr Johnson. I know that similar private associations would not justify my sending them to another favourite place of pilgrimage of my boyhood. No one to my knowledge, outside the Black Country, ever goes to the Clent Hills, which lie on its southern edge. There's little reason why anyone should; as hills, they are not much. But on the flank of one of them in St Kenelm's Chapel. If you don't know Clent you are unlikely to know St Kenelm; he scarcely exists in the hagiographies. He was a boy-king of Mercia who was murdered on the spot where the chapel, which is tiny and largely Saxon, now stands. To me as a boy, St Kenelm's was the shortest way back to the remote past of my England.

The only sensible advice to give one's foreign friends on what to see in Britain is the obvious advice. In London they must see the Abbey and St Paul's, the Houses of Parliament and Downing Street, the royal palaces and the pageantry. It would be absurd for them not to do so: they are tourists. The only test, when giving advice, is one's own behaviour abroad. He would be a pretty cold fish of an Englishman who visited Washington without at least staring at the White House, wandering through Georgetown and making the pilgrimage to Mount Vernon. And for tourists in Britain generally, well, the 'musts' are equally obvious: Oxford, Cambridge, Canterbury, Stratford, Salisbury, Winchester, Exeter, Coventry, Ripon, York, the Lakes, Edinburgh. . . . The list is endless.

For my own part, I find my own individual choices in the British scene are still dictated by my boyhood romanticism, except, of course, that home has become a different place. It is now London. Nothing deadens the responses like familiarity, and I have to have been away from England, and glutted with the exotic, before I can react as I used to to the south of England. I want other people to see it—the great skies of Romney Marsh, Rye and the Downs to the north and west, Brighton, the Isle of Wight, Lyme Regis and the whole county of Devon; but they have become too familiar to excite me as they did when I first descended on them from the smoke-stacked Midlands. They have become domesticated, and what permanently excites me are those places that are incapable of domestication, that exist, so to speak, in the context of worlds and time-scales utterly different from ours. In them, the ancient, even the.prehistoric earth obtrudes into the present like a granite outcrop. The largest of these timeless, untamed areas of Southern England is Dartmoor. Cars skim the roads that cross its surface, but still, in its wildness, its solitude, its sense of space, its exposure to extremes of climate, it exists outside our human pretensions.

In different ways, other places in the south of England do the same. Maiden Castle, outside Dorchester, Stonehenge, Glastonbury in Somerset, are man-made, but made by men so long ago and so remote from our ways of thinking as to be quite outside our era. By contrast with them, the medieval cathedrals of Britain, even the Roman remains, impress me as being of yesterday, and the English countryside as we normally know it the product of a few hours ago, for the English field system with its boundaries of hedges often does not go further back than the enclosures of the eighteenth century.

Maiden Castle, Stonehenge, Glastonbury are places of legend —of legend almost in default of history. The building of Stonehenge can be approximately dated, but why and how it was built are matters of conjecture. The legends that have accreted round these places are comparatively recent, but that is hardly relevant; their existence—and their invention—are testimonies of the spell the places themselves have laid on the imaginations of successive generations of men. Or take Glastonbury. The name is Saxon, but to the Britons the town was known as Avalon, the kingdom of the dead in Welsh mythology and in Arthurian romance the burial-place of King Arthur. The town, which is dominated by Glastonbury Tor, with the ruins of St Michael's Chapel on the top, stands in country reclaimed by the marshes of the River Brue. It was here, towards the end of last century, that the British lake village was discovered that provides us with the fullest information we possess about the way Britons lived at the time of the Roman conquest. But in addition the town also contains, besides fine medieval churches, the ruins of the great Benedictine abbey of St Mary. They date from the thirteenth century but stand on the site of a Norman monastery destroyed by fire in 1184. This is believed to have incorporated an earlier church built by St Dunstan in 942. Near it, also destroyed by the fire of 1184, was a little wattle church, which the medieval historian William of Malmesbury, writing about 1125, tells us was built in A.D. 125. A later legend, which William did not know, dates this wattle church even earlier and credits it to Joseph of Arimathea, from whose staff the Glastonbury Thorn, which flowers at Christmas as well as in the spring, is supposed to have sprung.

In all this we are in the realms of legend, and legends modern scholarship has pretty thoroughly disproved. Nevertheless, as I have said, they are not necessarily to be laughed at: where recorded history is a blank the imagination of men fills up the empty spaces. And what I find, at Stonehenge and Glastonbury in their different ways, is a quality making for awe in the beholder that I find nowhere else in Britain, the quality one feels, much more powerfully it is true, at Delphi and Nemi, a quality that in those places becomes numinous.

Whether I should have these feelings of awe if I approached Stonehenge and Glastonbury with a mind completely ignorant of the associations of history and legend in which they are steeped, I cannot possibly know. My feelings would certainly not be exactly the same, but I should, I believe, still be moved. Stonehenge and Glastonbury are as much part of their settings, their specific locations, as are Delphi and Nemi. The settings themselves strike one as works of genius, so that one could almost think it was they that produced the places for which they are famous. In any case, associations enhance. My response to Maiden Castle is the richer and the deeper because I first encountered it in the pages of *The Mayor of Casterbridge*. When I saw it myself I did so not only through my own eyes but also through Hardy's wiser and more penetrating eyes. And at Stonehenge, too, Hardy's Tess is now one of the unseen presences.

'God made the country, and man made the town': it is a typically eighteenth-century sentiment, and never was antithesis less true. Man made both. A nation's shrines, buildings, landscapes, ceremony and ritual are artifacts made by the men of that nation—and made not by their hands alone. Modern Scotland, by which I mean the notion of Scotland shared alike by the Scots and by the outside world, is the creation of Sir Walter Scott as much as any other single agency. The English Lake District is the work of the imagination of Wordsworth, in a sense the greatest poem he wrote. No doubt the Lakes can be appreciated by tourists who have not read a line he wrote; but I am sure that for their full appreciation a knowledge of his poetry is essential, for in a very real sense it was he who made the Lakes sublime.

The landscape of Britain, together with its towns and buildings, its memorable places, is at once the palimpsest of its history, recording the imprints upon it of successive generations of men, and the creation, too, of individual men. The roll-call of these men is largely the history of British art and literature. It is through their eyes that I, as a tourist, want to interpret the palimpsest of Britain.

Walter Allen

Parliament Square, London

As much as any, this view symbolises Britain. In the centre rises the Clock Tower, crowned by the face of Big Ben, while to the right are some of the buildings of the Houses of Parliament, collectively known as the Palace of Westminster. A disastrous fire in 1834 destroyed all of the original Palace except Westminster Hall, begun by William Rufus in the eleventh century. Sir Charles Barry's familiar Gothic-Revival design incorporated the surviving Westminster Hall, but, that apart, its apparent antiquity is not much more than a century old. The statue in the line of the Clock Tower commemorates Field-Marshal Smuts and is by Jacob Epstein. That to the left, by Thomas Woolner, is of Lord Palmerston.

(Overleaf) The Houses of Parliament

Like the picture on the facing page, this panorama could provide a national trade mark for Britain. The buildings it shows, themselves epitomise much of Britain's history. On the left can be seen the eighteenth-century towers of the medieval Westminster Abbey, in the centre, across the Thames are the turrets and pinnacles of the Houses of Parliament, next Westminster Bridge crosses the river, while to the far right is the Tudor gateway of Lambeth Palace, the official residence of the Archbishop of Canterbury.

The Tower of London and Tower Bridge

This third London view is as instantly recognisable as its predecessors. The Tower of London has been a key fortress of the city at least since Roman times: the four-square, turreted building in the centre of the picture is William the Conqueror's White Tower. To its right is the familiar outline of Tower Bridge; erected between 1886 and 1894, its 'bascules', along which the roadway normally runs, can be raised to allow ocean-going vessels to pass beneath to their moorings as far upstream as Kingston in Surrey.

30

St Paul's Cathedral, London

While surrounding buildings were turned into rubble in World War II, and have in many cases been permanently cleared away, the Cathedral itself was miraculously preserved. Indeed some aspects, like this one, are now better seen than they had ever previously been. St Paul's was of course designed by Sir Christopher Wren and was built, between 1675 and 1710, on the site of its medieval predecessor. Having supervised its erection and decoration over a period of thirty-five years, Wren himself survived as an old man of seventy-nine to witness the completion of his masterpiece.

Trafalgar Square, London

The visitors rest in the sun, watch the fountains or feed the pigeons; behind them rise the façades of two of London's most famous buildings: the National Gallery and St Martin-in-the-Fields. The National Gallery, which was built by William Wilkins in 1832–38, now houses one of the half dozen most remarkable collections of paintings in the world. St Martin's was designed a century earlier by James Gibbs. American visitors recognise it as the prototype on which many of their own New England churches were based.

Westminster Abbey, London

The Abbey is England's most historic church. It is here that her kings and queens have for centuries been crowned and here that many of her most famous men and women have been buried. Originally part of the buildings of a monastery, the Abbey was rebuilt in the eleventh century by Edward the Confessor. Additions and reconstructions have been made in every succeeding century. The North Transept, here illustrated, dates from about 1245-60; the stained glass in the rose window was added by Wren in the early eighteenth century.

36

Horse Guards Parade, London

Just as the Royal Guards protect the Amalienborg Palace at Copenhagen, so do the Household Cavalry, in equally archaic uniforms, form a personal bodyguard for the Monarch in London. Today their function is largely ceremonial—until, that is, there is a need for their more active employment as armoured fighting troops. At the State Opening of Parliament, and on similar royal occasions, the Household Cavalry provides a mounted escort for the Sovereign. Every week-day at eleven, however, and on Sundays at ten, they can be seen at the Guard-mounting ceremony, shown in this picture, on the parade ground behind the Horse Guards building in Whitehall.

Hampton Court Palace: The King's Privy Garden

The original palace of Hampton Court was built for Cardinal Wolsey in the early sixteenth century and presented, not without some cogent hints, to his royal master, Henry VIII. Henry added to the buildings, and so, with the help of Sir Christopher Wren, did a later monarch, William III, in the years 1689-94. With its extensive façades, formal gardens and radiating canals, Hampton Court represents England's nearest approach to a palace in the grand manner, such as Versailles. The Privy Garden here illustrated, belonged to Henry VIII's palace, but a part of the walls is all that now remains of its Tudor lay-out.

40

Windsor Castle, Berkshire

There has always been a variety of royal residences in Britain—Buckingham Palace in London, for instance, Balmoral in Scotland, Sandringham in Norfolk—but it is at Windsor that the monarch has latterly spent most time. The situation beside the Thames, the seclusion, and the nearness of London, have made it attractive, as has the Park, whether formerly for hunting or more recently for its polo ground. William the Conqueror built the original castle as a fortress and the Round Tower seen in this picture in fact dates from Norman times. The effect of the skyline is, however, largely an early nineteenth-century creation since the silhouette of the buildings was a piece of picturesque scene-painting by Sir Jeffrey Wyatville in the years immediately after 1824.

42

Arundel Castle, Sussex

Just as Windsor Castle stands guard over a stretch of the Thames, so does Arundel Castle lie above a loop of the river Arun in Sussex. There it has remained, at first a fortress, later a dwelling, in the centuries since its foundation during the decades after the Norman Conquest. Its early form, of mound and fort surrounded by a defensive wall, can, as at Windsor, still be distinguished amongst the extensive additions of succeeding centuries. Arundel Castle is the seat of England's premier nobleman, the Duke of Norfolk.

44

Sompting Church, Sussex

A country church separate from its village is common enough in England, but few indeed of those that remain are as old as Sompting. For nearly 900 years the strangely shaped tower, with its characteristic Saxon 'pilaster strips', has stood as a relic of the England which existed before the coming of the Normans. Not only the tower is Saxon: inside are remains of a frieze and wall arcade, and scraps of primitive carving, which were also a part of the remote, pre-Conquest church.

47

The South Downs, Sussex

In the foreground is the village of Milton Street, behind is a stretch of the Downland whose rounded chalk formation is seen in many other counties besides Sussex: Wiltshire and Berkshire to the west, for instance, or, north of London, in Bedfordshire and Hertfordshire. Often the chalk itself appears and sometimes the shallow soil has been cleared away in the shape of figures or horses on the hillside; some of them, like the White Horse at Uffington in Berkshire, are prehistoric in origin. To walk along the ridge of the Downs is to realise how much of England still remains rural and unspoiled.

The Seven Sisters, Sussex

This is how the Downs look when they reach the coast. Abruptly
they end in the shape of the white chalk cliffs, the sight of which
is so reassuringly familiar to the visitor approaching Dover from
the sea. This particular stretch lies between Eastbourne and Sea-
ford. Chalk is friable, so imperceptibly the Seven Sisters recede
as the action of sea and weather erodes them. Here they are preserved from housing development, and the impressive walk along
their edge should be enjoyed in the future as much as it is today.

Kentish Oast-Houses

Although the hops with which beer is flavoured are grown in other counties also, the oast-houses used for hops in Kent are peculiar to the county. For this reason most English people, if set down blind-folded in Kent, would have no difficulty in quickly discovering their whereabouts once the bandage was removed. This pair of oast-houses, set beside an equally characteristic weather-boarded farmhouse, is situated near Tunbridge Wells. 'Georgian', announce the glazing bars of the windows, and the admirable symmetry of the architecture indeed suggests an eighteenth-century date.

Tenterden, Kent

Wool was the foundation of England's prosperity during the later middle ages and—witness the substantial fifteenth-century church tower—it was wool which provided the wealth for the building of Tenterden. The houses shown in the picture, however, belong to the last two centuries, a period when Tenterden's importance had changed to that of a small market town. Today there has been a further shift of emphasis whereby Tenterden has become a shopping centre for families who live round about and whose wage-earners may travel daily to London.

55

Knole House, Sevenoaks, Kent

It was about the year 1600 that the building of Knole began. Its courtyards and wings and outbuildings grew to such an extent that, as the seventeenth century passed, Knole took on the size and self-sufficiency of a small town. Today its vast extent is still as great as that of one of the larger Oxford or Cambridge Colleges. Knole has for long been the seat of the Sackville family, one of whom, Vita Sackville-West, has left in *The Edwardians* a memorable account of life in the great mansion some sixty years ago.

Canterbury Cathedral, Kent

The camera looks down on the corona (1175–84) and on the tomb of the Black Prince (died 1376). Canterbury Cathedral is the mother church of England. A disastrous fire in 1174 gutted the earlier Norman building, and first William of Sens and after his death William 'the Englishman' were responsible for a new church. The work they began was continued through the centuries and finally crowned by the magnificent central tower of William Wastell (1493–97). Throughout the middle ages the Cathedral was the goal of pilgrims, from all over Europe, to the tomb of the martyred Thomas à Beckett.

Salisbury Cathedral, Wiltshire

Two features make Salisbury unique amongst medieval English cathedrals: it has the tallest spire (404 feet) and it was built predominantly in a single style and period (the 'Early English' of the mid-thirteenth century). This view shows the west front (1258–66) and the tower, begun by Richard Farleigh in 1334. The buildings round the wide and peaceful 'close' have been described as 'an epitome of English house design at its best periods'. John Constable, who used to stay at Salisbury with his friend and patron Archdeacon Fisher, left many pictorial memories of his love for the Cathedral.

Stonehenge, Wiltshire

A few miles west of Amesbury, on the border of Salisbury Plain, lies Stonehenge, a monument which vies with Carnac in Brittany as being the most extraordinary of the New Stone Age. The giant monoliths of which the stone circles are made up, have been smoothed and shaped, and some have been brought, by inconceivable effort, from as far away as Wales. For what precise purpose the prehistoric Celts erected Stonehenge is not known, and doubtless never will be, but it is reasonably conjectured that the significance was religious.

Lansdown Crescent, Bath, Avon

Bath, in Avon, is England's finest piece of eighteenth-century town planning. Set on the slope of a combe, crescents, streets, squares and terraces rise one above another in orderly magnificence. Lansdown Crescent was designed by John Palmer and built, comparatively late in Bath's development, between 1789 and 1793. The medicinal properties of Bath's chalybeate water were valued by the Romans, but it was Richard Nash (1674–1762) who established the spa as a resort of Georgian society: with what success the contemporary novels of Tobias Smollett and Jane Austen clearly show.

Gloucester Cathedral

To the right, at the east end of the cathedral, is the immense window of the lady chapel (1457–83), behind it lies the choir (1337–50), and above the crossing rises the central tower (1450–60). The beginnings of the cathedral are, however, much earlier than these dates suggest. In A.D. 681 a Benedictine abbey was founded at Gloucester. Nothing of that edifice remains, but the present building is conspicuous for the solemn strength of its Norman nave (1120–60). To the architectural historian the cathedral is significant because in it appeared for the first time the Perpendicular style which was England's contribution to medieval building.

Corfe Castle, Dorset

The village of Corfe is as pretty as a postcard, the castle behind as stark and uncompromising as its history. The castle's keep and inner bailey were built in the twelfth century, but their effectiveness was not fully put to the test for another 500 years. It was in 1643, during the Civil Wars, that Lady Banks conducted a prolonged and successful defence against the assaults of the Roundheads. Three years later the castle was taken as a result of the treachery of one of its defenders, and subsequent charges of gunpowder reduced it to the gaunt ruin which survives today.

St Michael's Mount, Cornwall

St Michael's Mount not only looks like Mont St Michel, it was actually named after its counterpart in Normandy by Edward the Confessor, who founded here, in 1044, a 'cell' of the parent monastery in France. Both Mounts are also similar in that at high tide each is an island. Some of the buildings on St Michael's Mount were part of the fifteenth-century monastery, others belong to the last century. More surprising in such a setting is a Georgian Rococo-Gothic drawing-room, and paintings by Gainsborough, Zoffany and Opie. St Michael's Mount has since 1660 been the seat of the St Aubyn family.

St Ives, Cornwall

Still a fishing village, St Ives is now better known as a holiday resort on the north coast of Cornwall fifteen or so miles from Land's End. Behind the harbour rises the tower of the strangely named church of St Ia; built of granite in the early fifteenth century, its tower is some 120 feet in height. Fishermen and holiday-makers are associated with St Ives; it has also for long been the centre of a school of artists, some of whom have become as internationally famous as Barbara Hepworth and Ben Nicholson.

72

Land's End, Cornwall

In Spain 'Cabo Finisterre', in Brittany the 'department of Finistère', in England the extremity of the earth became simply Land's End. On the day this picture was taken the sea was relatively calm. In a gale the waves from the Atlantic combine with powerful inshore currents to form a seething and deadly cauldron: one which can be a fearsome sight indeed from the deck of the small ship *Scillonian* on its passage from Penzance to St Mary's in the Scilly Isles.

Symond's Yat, Herefordshire

The river is the Wye and this particular stretch lies on the Welsh border, not far from the junction of Herefordshire, Gloucestershire and Monmouthshire. Fishermen and artists—notably Wilson Steer amongst the latter—have always valued the Wye for their differing reasons. 'Yat', incidentally, comes from the Old English word *geat*, here meaning valley, while 'Symond's' is a corruption of the 'Sigemund' with whom, more than a thousand years ago, the place was associated.

Tintern Abbey, Gwent

In a loop of the river Wye, ten miles or so downstream from Symond's Yat, are the ruins of Tintern Abbey. Wordsworth, like the Cistercians who founded the abbey in the twelfth century, was more impressed perhaps than we may be by the

> *steep and lofty cliffs,*
> *That on a wild secluded scene impress*
> *Thoughts of more deep seclusion.*

To the Cistercians remoteness was a necessary condition for a site of one of their monasteries and six hundred years ago Tintern possessed this quality as much as did the mother foundation of Cîteaux in France.

Castle Combe, Wiltshire

In the north of Wiltshire, not far from Chippenham, lies Castle Combe, one of the many villages which have been called 'the prettiest in England'. The claim of Castle Combe to this title is not easily gainsaid. The little river, the fifteenth-century church, the ochre houses with their grey stone slate roofs—all this, set against the steep beech woods of the combe itself, make up an unspoiled unity which, of its type, has few rivals in England.

Blenheim Palace, Oxfordshire

Like so much of the English landscape, this scene, apparently so natural, is really the result of art. The Palace itself was built (1705–20), in that most artificial of styles, the baroque, by Sir John Vanbrugh; the park was transformed in the eighteenth century by the tree-planting and lay-out of Lancelot ('Capability') Brown; even the lake is a creation more of man than of nature. Blenheim Palace was presented by the nation to the first Duke of Marlborough and commemorates his greatest victory. The Palace is scarcely less memorable as the birthplace of Sir Winston Churchill.

Oriel Street, Oxford

At the end of Oriel Street rises the spire of St Mary's, the University church, and to the right is a stretch of Oriel College. The undergraduates with the traditionally battered bicycles are 'commoners'; the black gowns they are wearing would be less abbreviated if they were scholars. No one knows more than approximately when either the City or the University was founded. Oxford is mentioned first in the *Anglo-Saxon Chronicle*, while the University seems to have been established in the eleventh century when English students, many of whom had earlier gone to Paris, began to settle in Oxford.

Stratford-on-Avon, Warwickshire

Much of Stratford now unfortunately looks so spurious that it is sometimes difficult to credit the town's real antiquity. Shakespeare, none the less, *was* born here, his monument and grave *can* still be seen in the parish church, and many of the buildings, however speculative their association with the poet, do undoubtedly survive from his day. For many people the incentive for a visit to Stratford is, however, less Shakespeare's association with the town than the outstandingly excellent performances of his plays at the Memorial Theatre.

King's College, Cambridge

In the spring the crocuses appear along the Backs, the under-graduates lie in the sunshine beside the Cam, and the buildings of King's and Clare look their finest. The west end of King's College Chapel (1446-1515) can here be seen at its full extent. To the right is the Fellows' Building (1723-29) which was designed by James Gibbs and which consequently is still more commonly known as the Gibbs Building. At the other side of the chapel is a second aspect of the same range of Clare seen in the previous picture.

Kersey, Suffolk

There can be no secret as to the source of Kersey's air of well-ordered prosperity. Just as Worsted in the next county of Norfolk gave its name to a kind of woollen material, so the twilled woollen cloth known as kerseymere was associated with the handsome village in the picture. Although, surprisingly, the word kerseymere has been in use only since the end of the eighteenth century, the wealth of the village had a much earlier date. The size and decoration of the roof and porch of the church alone attest that, at least since the fifteenth century, the wool trade had brought money to Kersey's merchants.

Elm Hill, Norwich, Norfolk

More than 30 English cities are today larger than Norwich, but during the middle ages, after Bristol and for part of the time York also, it was next to London the biggest town in Britain. Since then Norwich's decline has been relative only. In itself the city has maintained a steady prosperity and this picture reflects the architectural form which that prosperity took in the seventeenth century. 'There is not a single house in Elm Hill which could be disturbing,' remarked Professor Pevsner, and there is not one, we might add, which should be disturbed.

The Norfolk Broads

The river is the Ant, the scene is at Ludham Bridge, but judging simply from the pleasure boats, the flat countryside and the remains of the windmill, the view could as well be one of a score of other Broadland places. The Broads have existed since pre-historic times. They consist of a series of shallow meres, more or less extensive, often connected by such rivers as the Yare, the Bure, the Wensum and the Ant, and they are situated between Norwich and the north-west coast of the county. The Broads are said to be slowly filling up; in the meantime they provide the finest extent of water in England for safe sailing and cruising.

Bamburgh Castle, Northumberland

Six miles south from Lindisfarne along the Northumberland coast lies the village of Bamburgh, overshadowed by its tremendous castle. The *Anglo-Saxon Chronicle* claims that in A.D. 547 Ida, king of Northumbria, 'built Bebhamburh, which was first enclosed by a hedge and afterwards by a wall'. The buildings that survive today are a great deal more recent, indeed many are latter-day reconstructions: not the keep, however, whose area (69 feet by 61 feet) places it second only to Dover in the scale of Norman fortifications of the twelfth century.

York Minster

This is the east end of the Minster. The immense fifteenth-century window contains the greatest single area of contemporary stained glass in Europe. To the right is the chapter house, octagonal in shape and built between 1290 and 1310. York was at one time the capital of England; it was then, about the year A.D. 625, that the first cathedral of York was founded. Nothing remains from those early days, for the present cathedral is exclusively Gothic. In at least two respects it is one of the most remarkable in England: the height and span of the nave (1291-1345), and the exceptionally large amount of its surviving medieval stained glass.

Richmond, Yorkshire

There are five Richmonds in the British Isles. This one lies on the river Swale in Yorkshire, about fifteen miles south-west of Darlington. It is a little market town of less than 10,000 inhabitants, but it has been established for more than a thousand years. A castle, built not long after the Norman Conquest, stands on the summit of a rocky escarpment, its massive keep dominating the town. Richmond itself is as peaceful as its picture; the wide market place, cobbled hilly streets, fortifications and medieval church convey a continuing impression of the Richmond of earlier centuries.

Ashness Bridge, Cumberland

Little stone bridges, like this one at Ashness, near Keswick, frequently span the tumbling waters of the Lakeland becks. These bridges are generally narrow because they were first made for pack-ponies rather than wheeled traffic. The mountain in the distance is Skiddaw, at 3,054 feet one of the highest in the Lake District, and beneath it are the wooded shores of Derwentwater. The district is one closely associated with the Lake poets; Coleridge, indeed, called one of his sons after the river, the Derwent, which flows through the lake.

Derwentwater, Cumberland

This is a close-up of the lake distantly visible in the previous picture. Woods, little islands and surrounding hills whose tops, as on this day, are not infrequently hidden by cloud, are the features of Derwentwater. One of these hills is the unforgettably named Catbells which achieves literary immortality through being mentioned in Beatrix Potter's *Tale of Mrs Tiggy-Winkle*. Another association with literature occurs in *The Seven Lamps of Architecture*, where Ruskin says that his earliest recollection was of being taken by his nurse to Friar's Bray on Derwentwater.

Hadrian's Wall, Northumberland

Hadrian, it is said, built this wall, but of course we may be sure that those who really did the work were the Britons themselves, labouring under the watchful eyes of the Roman legionaries. The construction in any event was intended for permanence and has achieved it. In the years about A.D. 122–6 this tremendous defensive work, joining the seventy-four miles between Tyne and Solway, was put up as a protection for the peaceful South against marauding attacks from the North. For two and a half centuries, until the departure of the Romans from Britain, the Wall continued successfully to fulfil its function. This view is of the section near Housesteads, one of the forts in which the defending legionaries were stationed.

Harlech Castle, Gwynedd

It did not take long to build Harlech Castle: only half a dozen years during the eighties of the thirteenth century. What is clear, however, is the success with which Harlech could fulfil its purpose of an impregnable base from which the potentially hostile Welsh could be kept in subjugation. Four-square, Harlech stands on its rocky eminence, astonishingly little altered by any damage which enemies or weather could effect during the intervening centuries. Behind it the sea, Harlech here looks across to the Cambrian Hills.

Melindwr Valley, Dyfed

For an island which is one of the most thickly populated in the world, Britain constantly surprises the visitor by the tracts of country in which there are scarcely any people. In much of the Scottish Highlands, for instance, the population of deer exceeds that of human beings, and in parts of Snowdonia one can walk on the hills for a day and see only one or two other men or women. Cardiganshire, by these standards, is a great deal less empty of people, for in the parish of Melindwr, of which this seemingly empty valley forms a part, there are nearly 600 souls (albeit spread over more than 8,000 acres).

Caernarvon Castle

Caernarvon is in North Wales and this castle was built there by Edward I to protect his dominion in the uncertainly-held Principality. Looking at the steadfast exterior of the walls, it requires an effort of the imagination to realise that here they have been, not so very different, at any time since their completion in the year 1323. From the military historian's viewpoint Caernarvon is important because, with Conway (also built by Edward), it provides the outstanding example of that new type of castle whose strength lay in the single circuit of its tower-studded walls.

Edinburgh

One of the most extensive panoramas of Edinburgh is that to be had from Calton Hill, the site from which this picture was taken. To the left, beneath the Castle, are the wynds and lands of the Old Town; down the centre runs the line of Princes Street punctuated by the nineteenth-century fantasy of the Scott Memorial; to the right, behind the monument to Dugald Stewart, are the Georgian squares, crescents and terraces of the New Town. (Dugald Stewart, incidentally, although today forgotten, once enjoyed a European reputation as a professor of moral philosophy.)

Edinburgh castle

Above the corbie-stepped gables of the Grassmarket rises the most dramatic piece of townscape in Britain: Edinburgh Castle. *Dun Edin*, the 'fortress on the slope', was the name the Picts gave the original fort more than 1500 years ago—a suffix which later formed the initial element in the name of the town which grew around its base. The earliest surviving part of the present Castle, St Margaret's Chapel, dates from 1076 and is still in use for worship. Nowadays the Castle continues to stand, more than any other building, as representative of Edinburgh itself. In recent years it has won an additional fame as an un-matched setting for the Military Tattoo which has for so long formed the highlight of the annual Festival.

Loch Earn, Perthshire

Loch Earn is one of those deep, fresh-water lochs which, no matter how low the temperature, remains unfrozen throughout the winter. This picture was taken at its eastern extremity near the village of St Fillans. The name of the village commemorates a Celtic saint who was the evangelist of all this part of Scotland. In the middle ages his relics were believed capable of working miracles. Robert the Bruce ascribed his victory over Edward II at Bannockburn (1314) to the fact that an arm bone of St Fillan had been carried into battle as a sacred talisman.

Loch Lomond, Strathclyde

The biggest lake in Scotland, more than twenty-four miles long from north to south, Loch Lomond lies on the southern border of the Highlands yet near enough to Glasgow for an area at the southern end to be preserved by the Corporation as a park. The surrounding mountains, all of them considerable, culminate in the 3,192 feet of Ben Lomond. 'Bonny' the banks of the loch undoubtedly are, but they have seen some bloody fighting in their day between the two clans, Colquhoun and MacGregor, who lived on opposite shores.

Glencoe, Strathclyde

Glencoe looks the part. The steepness of its rocky and beetling sides insures that the valley itself is often in ominous shadow. A knowledge of the massacre which took place here on 13th February 1692 adds to the visitor's sense of doom. Glencoe had long been the home of the lawless MacDonalds. In order to make his peace with the Crown, the head of the clan took an oath of submission and loyalty. The resulting sense of security was the MacDonalds' undoing. Suddenly, at night, on treacherous orders from Secretary of State Stair, soldiers set upon the unsuspecting MacDonalds, burning their houses, destroying goods and cattle, and driving those they failed to murder into the cruel rigours of an unprotected Highland winter.

Eilean Donan, Ross and Cromarty

At the head of Loch Alsh, separated from the mainland by a causeway and bridge, is a fine example of that Scots vernacular style which the nineteenth century so widely travestied. Here is the 'Scots Baronial', with its defensive turrets, corbie-stepped gables and high walls pierced by tiny windows—reconstructed, it is true, but in the spirit of the original. Primarily these castles were dwelling places, but the unruly nature of their times is reflected in the posture of defence which the architecture was compelled to assume. The little islet has a human history long preceding the castle: here St Donan built his church and here too in still earlier centuries a vitrified fort once stood.

Skye, Inverness-shire

The little settlement is Elgoll, the snow-covered peaks across the bay are those of the Cuillins. Skye with an area of some 670 square miles, is by far the largest of the Inner Hebrides. While it is undeniably as 'mountainous', 'indented' and 'very moist' as the gazetteer claims, for the visitor Skye will always remain, scenically, without a rival. The height of the Cuillins, its peaks over 3,000 feet, means that they are the most compelling feature of the island.

(Overleaf) Castle Stalcaire, Strathclyde

In Gaelic the name of Castle Stalcaire (or Stalker) signifies Falconer's Castle—a reminder of the days when James IV of Scotland used it as a hunting lodge. The rocky island on which the Castle is situated is near the shore of Loch Laich at Portnacroish. Now a shell only, when its regal days were over Castle Stalcaire was for long the headquarters of the Stewarts of Appin. But at Culloden the clan supported the Young Pretender, the head of the clan was exiled, the building became ruinous, and now only the Royal Stewart arms over the Castle doorway remains to tell the reader of the tragic association between Prince Charles Edward and the family which bore the same name.